ISBN: 9798873396436
Published by Amazon.com

Created in Trinidad and Tobago

DEVOTION

EMOTION

MOTION

OCEAN

Poems inspired by the salt

waters and coastal zones

of the world

By Katrina Khan-Roberts

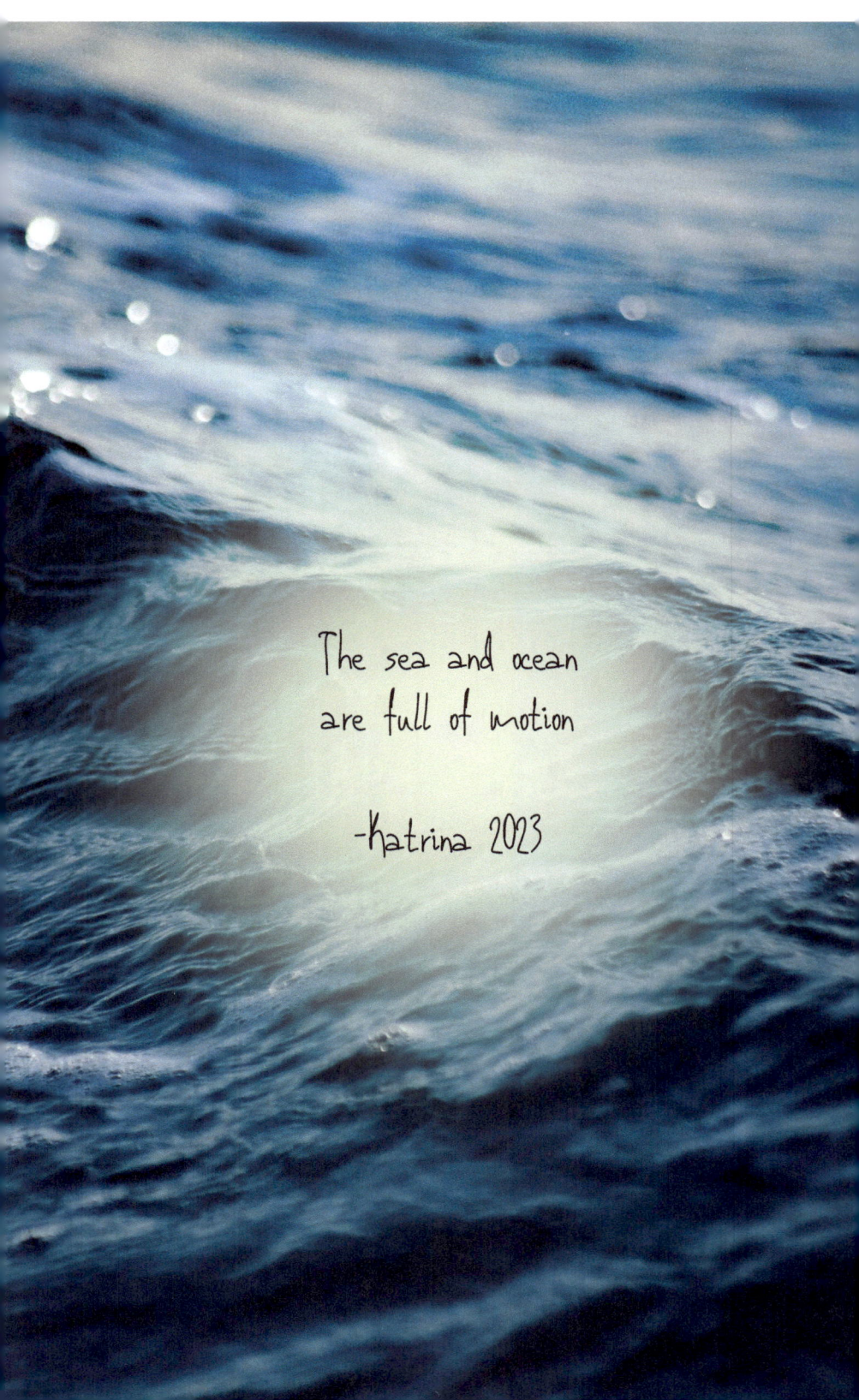

The sea and ocean
are full of motion

-Katrina 2023

This world we live on
Is green and blue,
The greatest depths of which,
We have yet to view.

Come with me as I wander,
In, around and through,
To connect science and emotions,
And present them here to you.

Water Chemistry

We see the sea and
sky as shades of blue,
Water supports life,
old and new.
Chemistry, Physics,
Biology all,
Moving together in
constant sprawl.

The vulnerable life on
this planet depends,
On this cycle we hope
never ends.
Through time we
spin, circling around,
Between the
atmosphere and the
ground.

Salt Water

A dense solution,
A salty soup,
The water in the ocean,
Moves in a loop.
It doesn't have a start,
Neither an end,
A support system for all,
From largest whale to krill to tend.
The salt water is healing,
A refuge for the soul,
Bringing inspiration and wonder,
With every wave roll.
A source of countless wonders,
A product of time,
With every beating heart,
Alive in rhythm and rhyme.

Water

Could a water droplet make a difference
To a river or a sea?
Could one voice sway the masses?
How could they see what I see?
But what if one droplet met another,
Observing the same trend,
Then others come together,
Flowing stronger with every friend.
The people of the marine states,
Indigenous, introduced, all,
See the plight of nature,
And are rising to the call.
Our watchwords in Trinidad and Tobago,
Together we aspire, together we achieve,
Personify how a few droplets,
Can help national mindsets interweave.
Often our natural resources,
Such as water are not appreciated.
Until they affect society directly,
These forces are underrated.

Floods ruin properties,
And cause breakouts of disease,
Erosion and landslides on the hills,
Have us falling to our knees.
We need rivers for our livelihoods,
No matter how far you may be.
Fresh water is used every day,
From the watershed to the sea.
Our rivers are full of flora and fauna,
Unique, native and alive,
But pollution and toxins are circulating,
Making it harder for them to thrive.
Our islands are surrounded by water,
Yet fresh water is alarmingly scarce,
And for something so basically needed,
The fight will become more fierce.
If youth holds the key to the future,
And droplets form the ocean and streams,
Then when we all come together,
Nothing can stop the realisation of our dreams.
So in the quest for water sustainability,
There is only one thing that's true,
To conserve this precious resource,
The responsibility lies with me and with you.

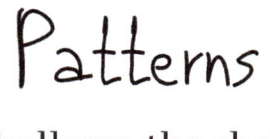

Patterns

The shallows, the shallows,
Where light shines through,
The swirling swash,
That traces patterns anew
In the shifting sediment,
By the swill of the tide,
Where I love to watch
The sea foam glide.

Lullaby Sea

Drift away

Drift away

Drift away on the waves of sleep.

Drift away

Drift away

Drift away to dreams so deep.

Float away

Float away

Float away on the peaceful tide.

Float away

Float away

Float away, your dreams will guide.

Cliffs

The power of water moving,
Is seen most clearly at the coast.
The place where forces meet,
Where erosion can happen the most.
Cliffs carved out of the headlands,
Towering above the salty mist,
A home for a range of creatures,
That is just too long to list.
Every crack and crevasse,
A pocket in which a life can live,
Birds, crustaceans and plants,
On the rock face that doesn't forgive.
A place of wind and weather,
A product of tectonics and time,
Exposed to the wild elements,
Always worth the climb.

Sea Birds

Soaring over the salty air,
Marine birds in flight.
They're specialists in many ways,
To survive the coastal day and night.

Oil glands and beaks with pockets,
Just to point out a few.
They come with every shape and feature,
In each and every hue.

Their vocals fill the spaces,
Between the sounds of splashing water.
Some of them even dive under them,
And take fish up to aerial slaughter.

There is nothing quite like seeing,
A marine bird flying high,
A shape to add to the ocean visuals,
As the sea melts into the sky.

Beach Life

Just as sea foam dances
on the waves,
And the ebb and flow over time
carves out the deepest caves,
So do the creatures
that live in the sand,
Take their time as part
of sea and land.

They are specialised in many ways,
To keep up with the changing days,
The swash and backwash and
shifting swill,
A dynamic environmnet
for their skill.

Hard shells and digging parts,
Multiple muscles and feeding arts,
The amazing world of the sea shore,
Is always a treasure trove to explore.

Tides

The tides of time,
Flowing in and out,
Moving unnoticed,
But spanning throughout,
The waters of the ocean,
All one big blue,
Connecting and linking,
Everything and you.

Echinoderm

Starfish, not a fish but an
Echinoderm you are,
Why did they name you a fish,
Though it's true you are like a star?
But lo! Your name goes not just with
five arms,
But as many as can be!
There are so many echinoderms
Living in the sea.

Brittle stars, sand dollars, urchins to
name a few,
And don't forget the sea cucumber
and others we never knew!
Classifications are something the
humans love to do,
But there is sometimes no point,
Because there are anomalies
through and through.

Seashells

Seashells, seashells on the shore,
Shapes and sizes and colours galore.
Made from a lifeform no longer inside.
A defence, a home, to shelter and hide.

What stories you keep in each layered line.
What was your life like until your time?
Now you have caught my wandering eye,
While my toes were in the sand, walking by.

Do you know your future as you lie in rest,
Being moved about by waves and tempest?
Will you bleach in the sun or be buried in
the sand?
Or will you be picked up by a
beachcombing hand?

Whatever you were and whatever is to be,
You will always belong to the sea.
Formed by salty life, part of other schemes,
I'll leave you to the coastline to do with you
what it deems.

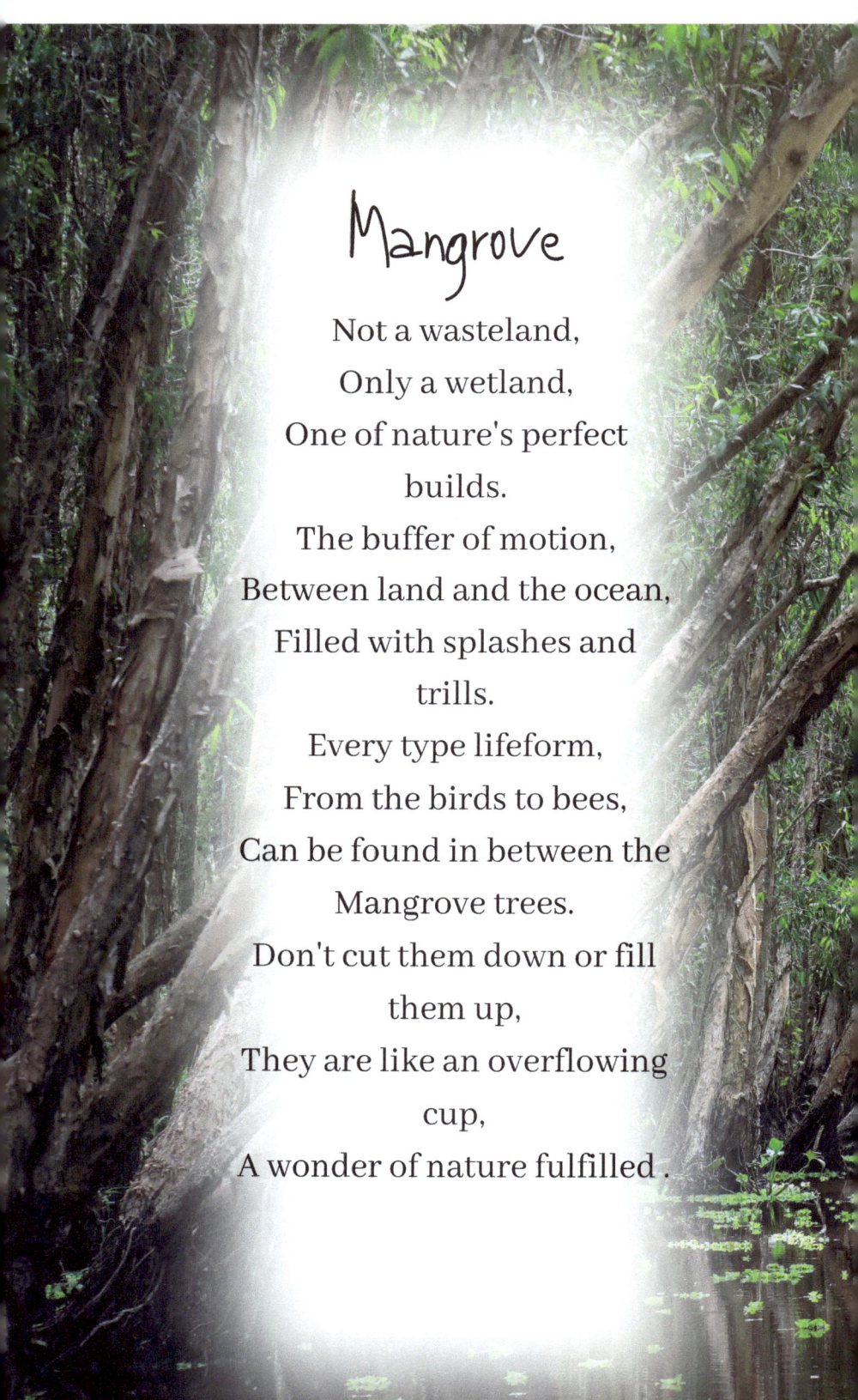

Mangrove

Not a wasteland,
Only a wetland,
One of nature's perfect
builds.
The buffer of motion,
Between land and the ocean,
Filled with splashes and
trills.
Every type lifeform,
From the birds to bees,
Can be found in between the
Mangrove trees.
Don't cut them down or fill
them up,
They are like an overflowing
cup,
A wonder of nature fulfilled .

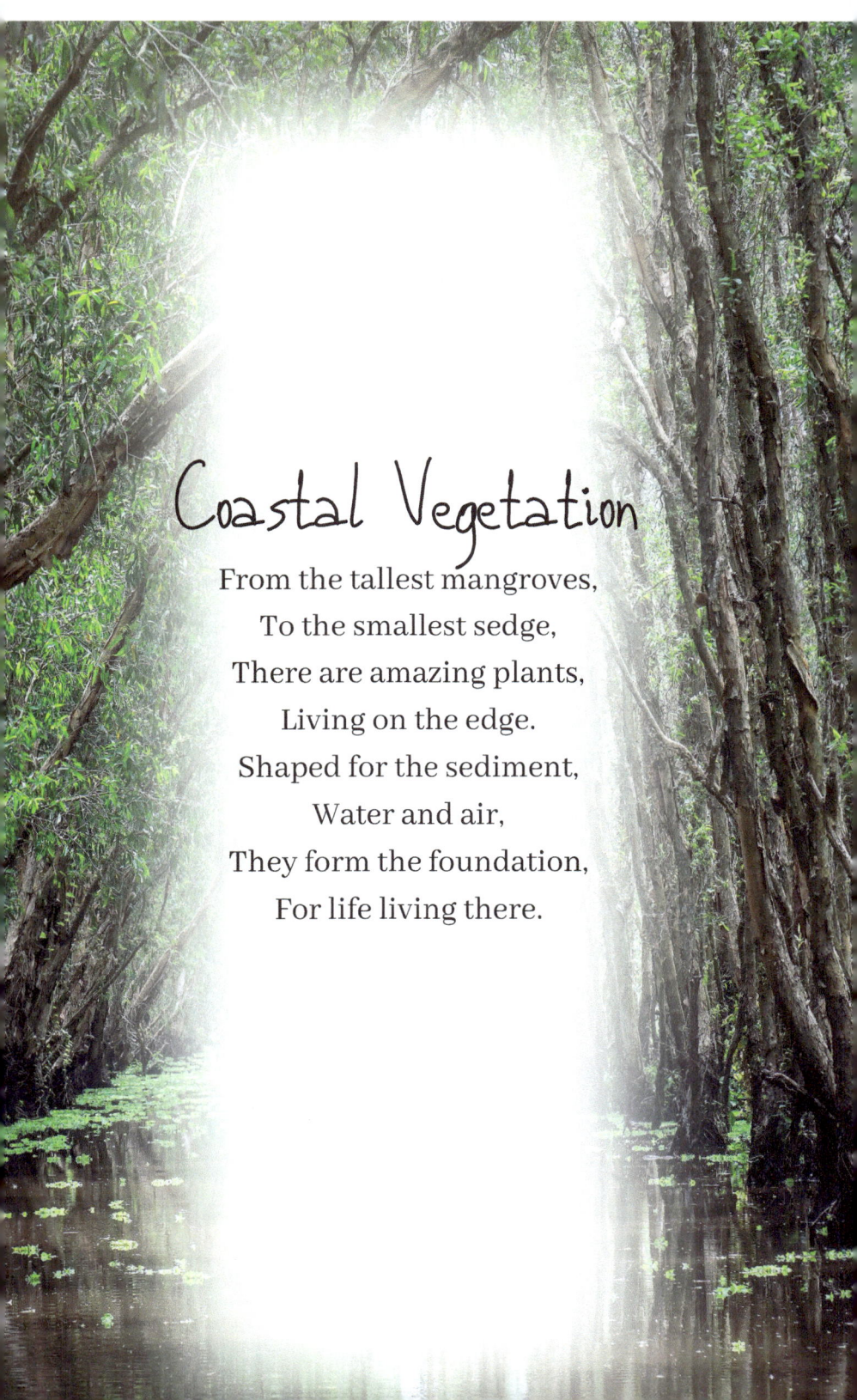

Coastal Vegetation

From the tallest mangroves,
To the smallest sedge,
There are amazing plants,
Living on the edge.
Shaped for the sediment,
Water and air,
They form the foundation,
For life living there.

Sea Grass

Wafting gently,
To and fro,
Fronds of grass,
But not exactly above as below.
In the brightly lit waters,
Salty and nutrient dense,
Photosynthesis in the shallow sea,
Gives this marine meadow presence.
Food for the fishes,
And the turtles mostly too.
A place of refuge for juveniles,
Before they venture into the blue.
Pollination, oh my,
A marine flowering plant.
Even more amazing,
Are the organisms they enchant.
So save the seagrass plains,
No matter shaped or sized.
They may be ticklish underfoot,
But their functions are prized.

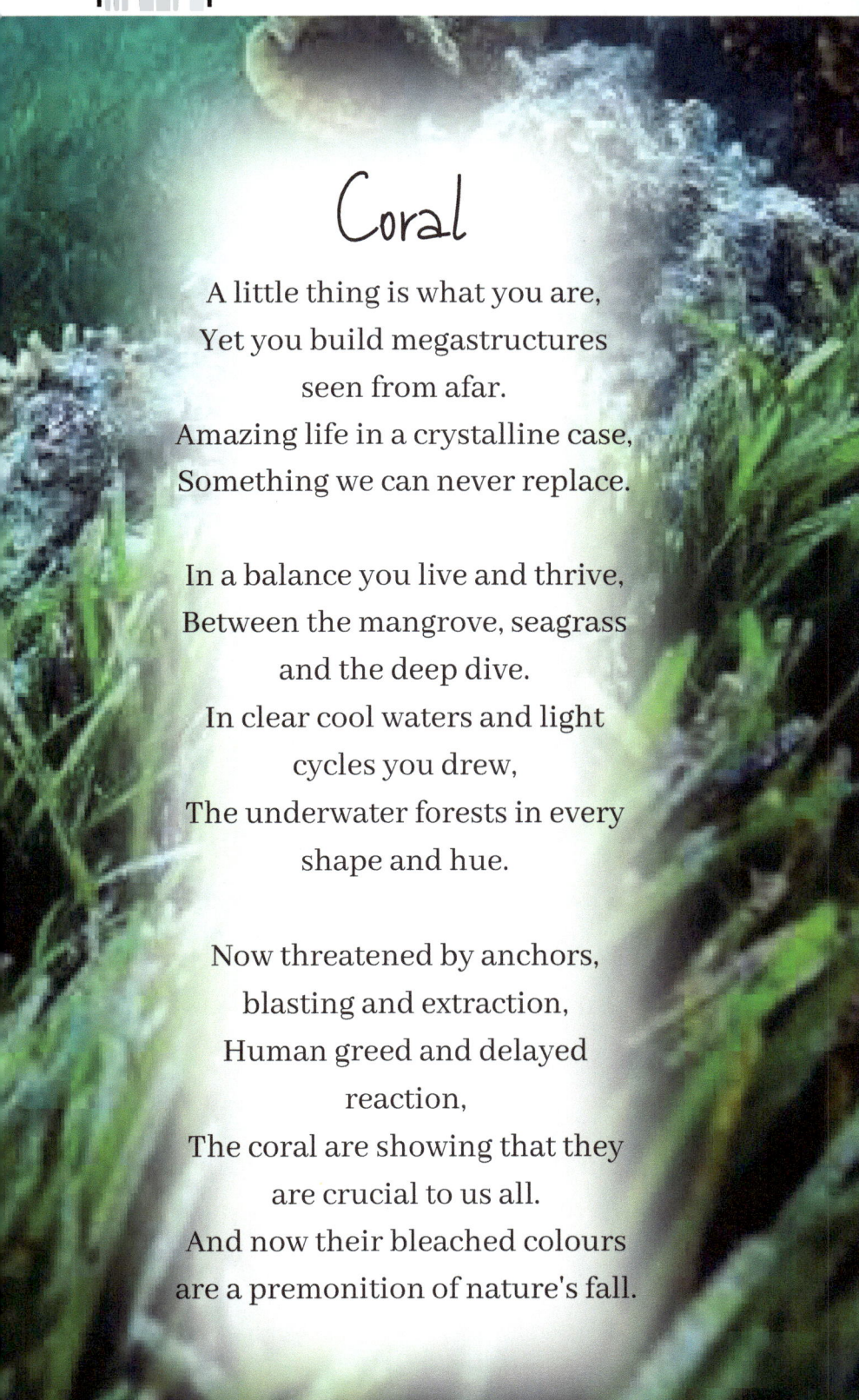

Coral

A little thing is what you are,
Yet you build megastructures
seen from afar.
Amazing life in a crystalline case,
Something we can never replace.

In a balance you live and thrive,
Between the mangrove, seagrass
and the deep dive.
In clear cool waters and light
cycles you drew,
The underwater forests in every
shape and hue.

Now threatened by anchors,
blasting and extraction,
Human greed and delayed
reaction,
The coral are showing that they
are crucial to us all.
And now their bleached colours
are a premonition of nature's fall.

Jellies

Where have the jellyfish gone?
I am sad because I know why.
They used to float just under the jetty,
And loved watching them wafting by.

Now there is nothing alive to watch,
While we bob before we sail.
All that's left is green water,
And the smell of something stale.

How can we expect the jellies to live,
If all we dump in the sea is waste?
How would you like it if all around you,
Was something toxic to smell and taste?

So I miss the jellies,
And think that once I'm gone,
There won't be anyone else to miss them,
Because most people don't pay attention as they
move along.

Sea Spray

The waters are whipped,
By the strong breeze,
Into a frenzy,
That moves the seas.
The salty soup,
Filled with minerals and life,
Are stirred to a frenzy,
And begins to look like a knife,
Is poking through the surface,
Causing it to protrude,
Peaks form valleys as the water rolls,
Surface tension overruled.
To the sky flies the freed spray,
Swept up by the wind.
Droplets refract the sunlight for a light display,
And in a moment the colours rescind.

Whales

Like a dream,
Drifting deeper;
Below the waves,
Deep sleeper.
With bottomless eyes,
Ardent abyss;
Holding a breath,
Pressure's kiss.
Giant on Earth,
Largest life;
Echos in song,
Throughout the strife.
Oh gentlest majesty,
Regally rare,
We are grateful for you,
Living out there.

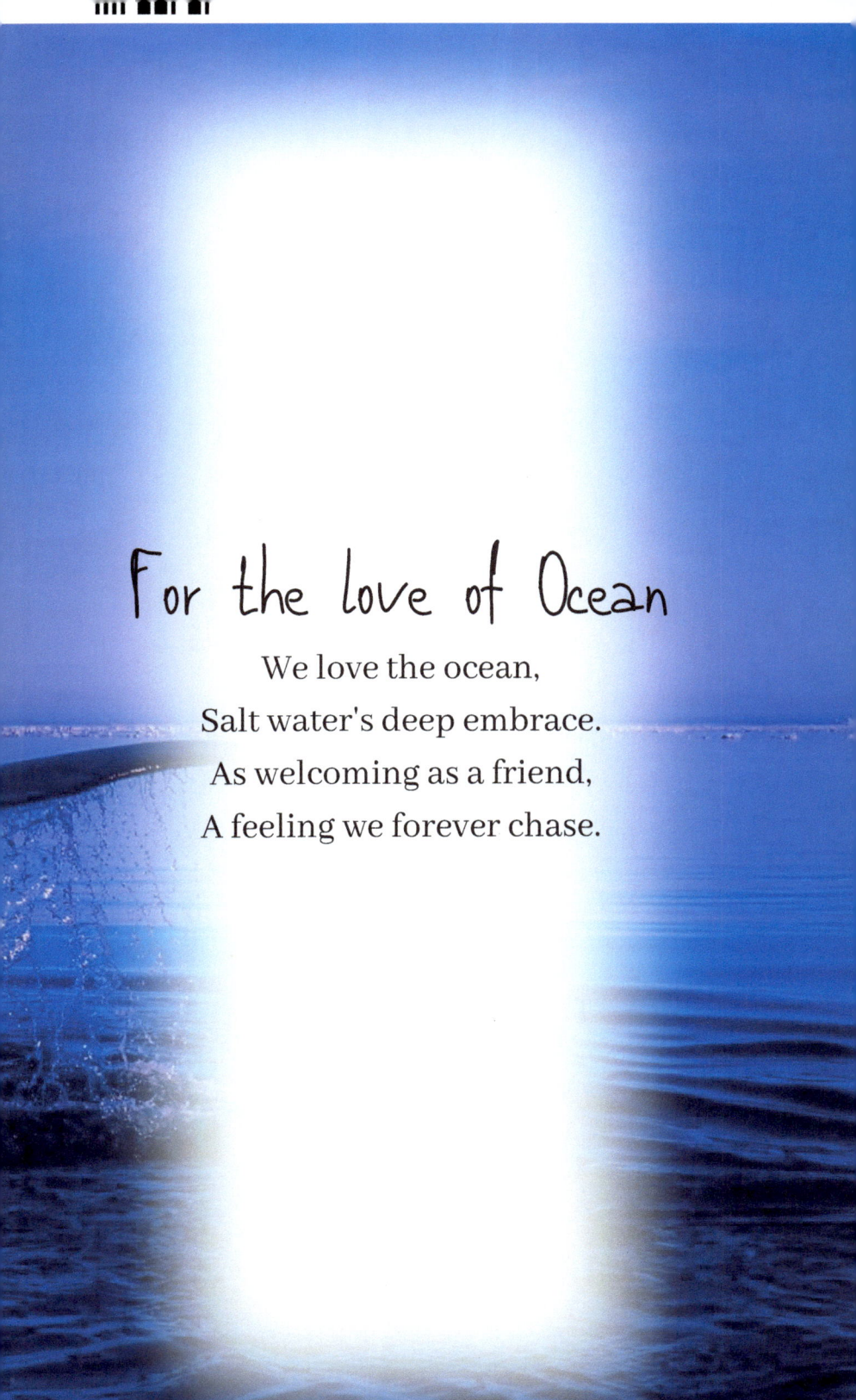

For the love of Ocean

We love the ocean,
Salt water's deep embrace.
As welcoming as a friend,
A feeling we forever chase.

Fish

The metallic flash of light
on scales,
As they twist and turn and
move their tails,
With flicking fins to propell
and guide,
As they navigate the sea so
wide.
A source of nourishment,
A living clue,
Detailing how lifeforms,
Evolved in the blue.
Precious resources,
That have been exploited
without care,
A wonder to think about,
Living quietly out there.

Fins

To move through water,
Dense sea water,
Something had to be formed.
To propell and push,
A directional push,
So the bodies transformed.

The fin, fused flesh,
Cartilage or bone under flesh,
To travel the Ocean wide.
Through the calm,
And not so calm,
To survive the changing tide.

Benthos

On the bottom of the ocean,
On the sea floor,
There is life undiscovered,
There is life that forms lore.

There is nothing less known,
Than the abyss of the sea,
In the dark and high pressure,
Specialisation is key.

They are flattened or soft,
They are reflective or colourful,
They are scavengers and rogues,
The deep sea is unknown and
wonderful.

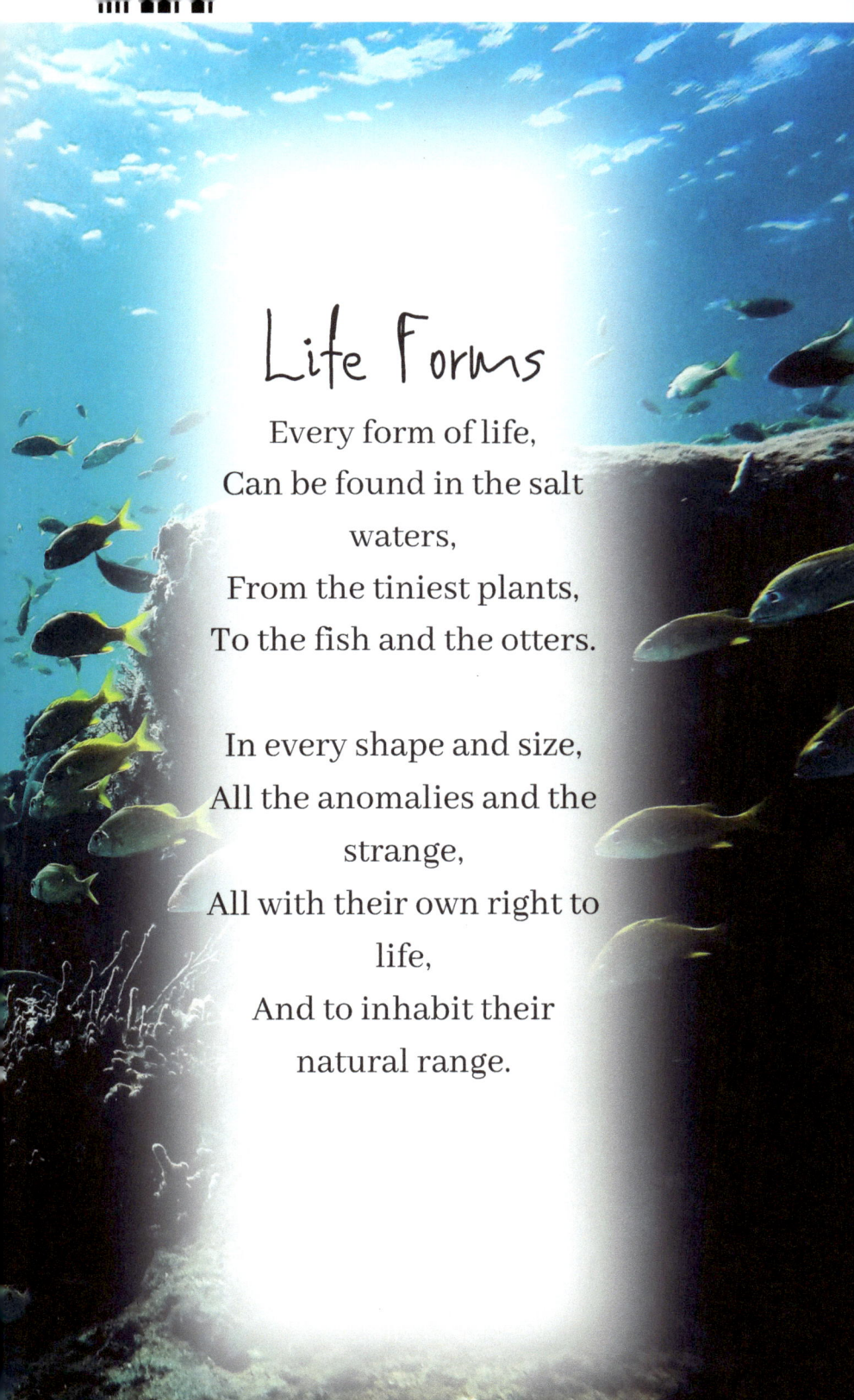

Life Forms

Every form of life,
Can be found in the salt
waters,
From the tiniest plants,
To the fish and the otters.

In every shape and size,
All the anomalies and the
strange,
All with their own right to
life,
And to inhabit their
natural range.

Deep Sea

Down,
Where the light can't reach,
Past where mammals,
Would dare to breech.
The largest environment,
On this planet,
Full of life,
In a harsh place to inhabit.
Shining skin,
Metal tinged,
Less oxygen,
Jaws unhinged.
Weird and wild,
Soft under pressure,
A magical wilderness,
Full of things to treasure.

Biolight

A glowing speck,
A flash of light,
Only visible,
In the deep darkness or night.

A chemical reaction,
A visceral call,
Bursting forth,
To shock and to stall.

A unique response,
A rare gift,
Dazzling and distracting,
Science and magic adrift.

Ocean Monsters

We know of the mermaids
The leviathan, the kraken,
The sea whip and the others of
the deep,
They have founded our dreams,
Our nightmares, our fears,
The unknown of the world that
out of the darkness could creep.
We do not know what is there,
And still yet we fear,
The deep darkeness that is vastly
unexplored,
But the few times we descended
We unceremoniously
ended
the natural draw of life's chord.
So leave the deep to the deep, the
dark to the dark,
let the monsters rest.
But who are the real monsters I'd
beg to ask,
I'd say the humans who invade
like a pest.

Mermaid

The waves are my playground,
The deep is my home.
I'm as free as a tuna,
Chasing a shoal,
But my home is at risk,
From a threat I can't reach.
From all of the people,
Exploiting the deep sea breach.
What do I do?
Where can I go?
No one can help me,
My voice is too low.
Please think of me down here,
And use your own cry,
Learn more about the ocean,
To make a change, just try.

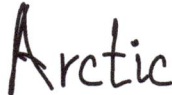

Arctic

The life of the arctic,
Where energy is scarce,
Where there is competition,
And fighting for resources is fierce.

Where everything is colourless,
And survival carries a higher price,
But still a place of wonder,
From the lifeforms to the ice.

Cold Seas

Some say they are empty,
Cold and devoid of life,
But the frosty seas of the North and South,
Have their share of wildlife.
As with everywhere else,
They are specialised and tough,
So they can flourish in the freezing,
And what little there is would be enough.
Mammals, birds, fish and more,
Can thrive within this space.
Adapting within the conditions,
The arctic is a wonderous place.

Coastal Sunsets

Sunset marks the end of the day,
A display of colours across the sky.
Refraction and reflection,
In every direction,
Made magic when wet meets dry.

Standing on the shoreline,
The sun hanging low,
An explosion around the sun,
Cut off by the horizon,
A wonder in the glow.

Sea Breeze

Salty and tangy,
Refreshing and a blessing,
Nothing quite compares,
To the sea breeze.
It whips up whitecaps,
Tickles the trees,
Shapes the sands,
All with ease.
The greater the fetch,
The greater the energy,
We can not fathom,
Its scale.
Moving the ocean,
The atmosphere,
All round,
A circuit difficult to derail.

Tempest

The signs of a storm coming ashore,
The tree branches are not moving the
way they were before.
A rage licks the waves high into the air,
And animals flee filled with wonder and
fear.
The vegetation is uprooted,
Plucked by the wind,
The rain hammers down,
All life is pinned
Down until it's all over,
By the loss of energy following any
protest,
And yet humans never listen,
To the voice of the tempest.

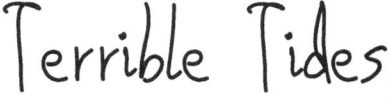

Terrible Tides

Truly torturous are the terrible
tides
They are tumultuous,
treacherous and testy besides.
Tempests and tidalwaves toss
the seep,
Tsunamis and storms turn the
shallows to deep.

Ocean

Just a little deeper,
Just beyond the waves,
The inky water calms,
And murmers through the
caves.

The quiet is settled and
constant,
The pressure is heavy and
defined,
The light ripples around
you,
A more perfect peace is
hard to find.

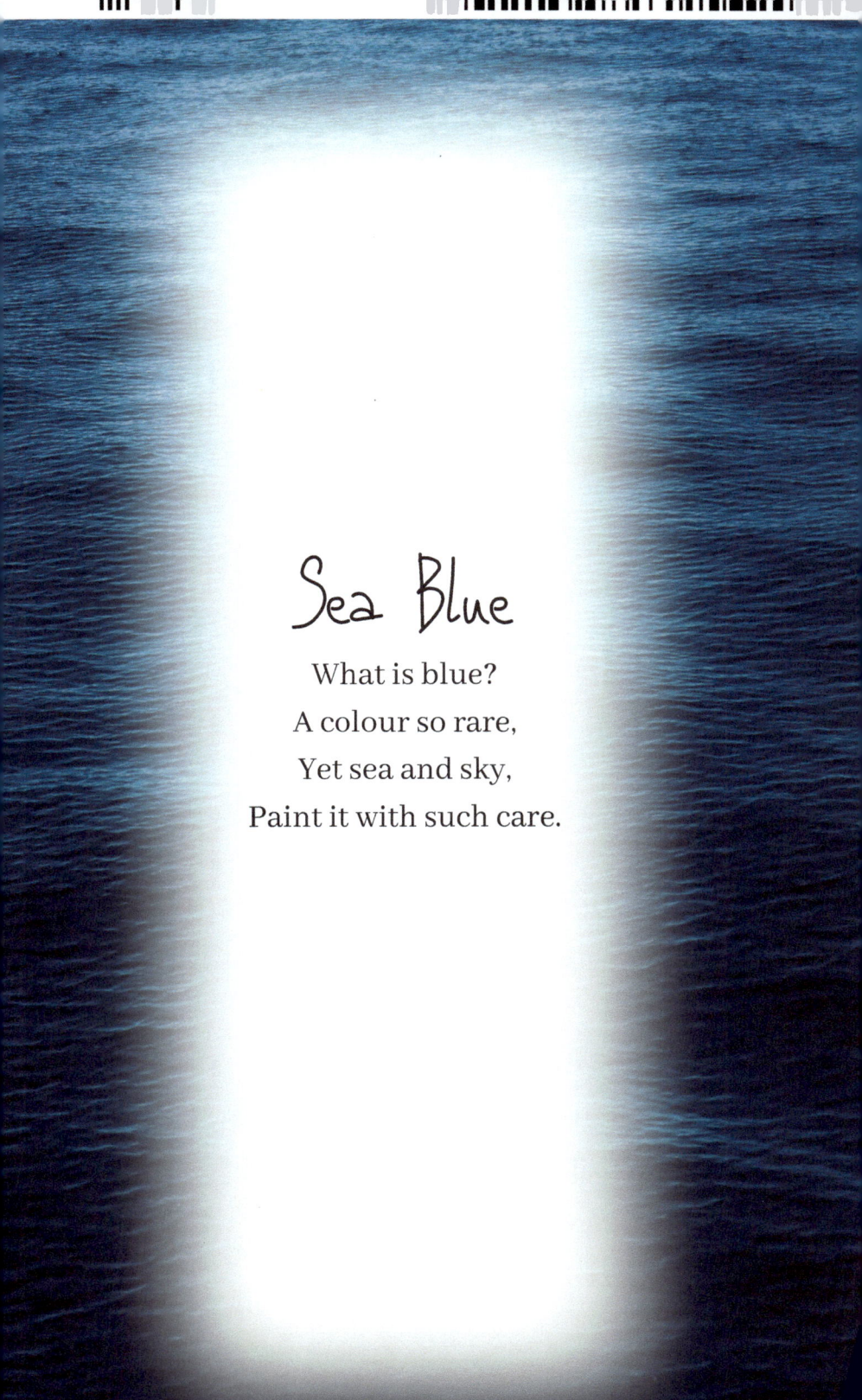

Sea Blue

What is blue?
A colour so rare,
Yet sea and sky,
Paint it with such care.

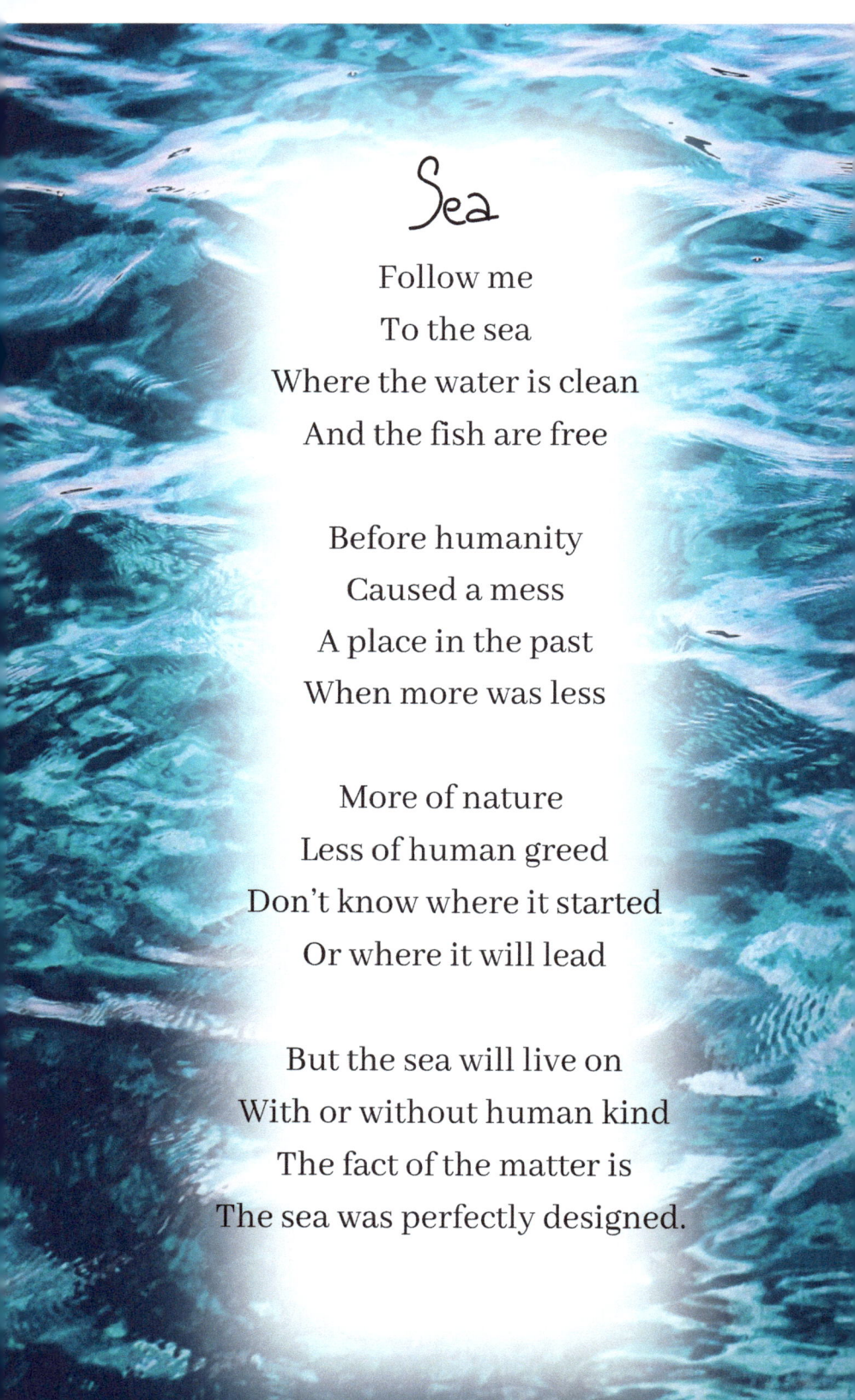

Sea

Follow me
To the sea
Where the water is clean
And the fish are free

Before humanity
Caused a mess
A place in the past
When more was less

More of nature
Less of human greed
Don't know where it started
Or where it will lead

But the sea will live on
With or without human kind
The fact of the matter is
The sea was perfectly designed.

Anthropocene

Bubble and tumble,
The ocean was new,
A great resource,
The great big blue.
The people saw it,
As a place for waste,
A dumping ground,
The tide would make space.
Fish were fished,
Whales were whaled,
People explored,
Sail they sailed.
The Ocean was pillaged,
Poisoned and plundered,
'Where is the treasure?'
The people wondered.
Only too late,
Do the people now see,
The treasure was the ocean,
All the wonders of the sea.

Caribbean Monk Seal

I was a gentle giant on the Caribbean shore,
Curious, I never saw humans like these before.
They were sailing along on their weird logs,
But these were the size of whales, not sea dogs.

I was lounging on the white Caribbean sand,
Curious, I observed them as they came on land.
With strange pointed sticks and woven mats
Dragging something else behind them with
shining slats.

I was lying in my own blood and blubber,
Curious, I wondered at the sounds of thunder.
There was no rain in the blue sky or on the seas,
While the humans brought extinction to my
species.

Void

What was once an ocean full of life
Is now an empty place
From a multitude of moving shapes
To a voided space.

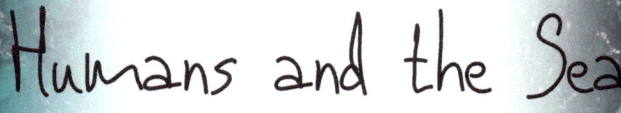

Humans and the Sea

Humans have lost the
concept,
Of stewardship and care,
When it comes to the sea,
We take for granted that it's
There,
Regulating our resources,
Services and ability to cope,
Not seeing our activities are
Throwing us out of scope.

Ocean Literacy

The ocean needs our assistance,
The sea needs our aid,
To manage everything that has happened,
Due to our human tirade.
For us to make it better,
First we learn about what was once was,
Then we understand how we got here,
See what doesn't work and what does.
We have to look through every lense,
See the problems from every side,
Then come together as one,
To sustainably and ethically guide.
We need to look to the future,
A united human race,
So we can protect the Ocean,
A stewardship we should never replace.